Congressional
Research
Service

Budget "Sequestration" and Selected Program Exemptions and Special Rules

Karen Spar, Coordinator
Specialist in Domestic Social Policy and Division Research Coordinator

October 2, 2012

Congressional Research Service

7-5700

www.crs.gov

R42050

Summary

"Sequestration" is a process of automatic, largely across-the-board spending reductions under which budgetary resources are permanently canceled to enforce certain budget policy goals. It was first authorized by the Balanced Budget and Emergency Deficit Control Act of 1985 (BBEDCA, Title II of P.L. 99-177, commonly known as the Gramm-Rudman-Hollings Act).

Sequestration is of current interest because it was included as an enforcement tool in the Budget Control Act of 2011 (BCA, P.L. 112-25). Sequestration can also occur under the Statutory Pay-As-You-Go Act of 2010 (Statutory PAYGO, Title I of P.L. 111-139). In either case, certain programs are exempt from sequestration, and special rules govern the effects of sequestration on others. Most of these provisions are found in Sections 255 and 256 of BBEDCA, as amended.

Two provisions were included in the BCA that could result in automatic sequestration:

- Establishment of discretionary spending limits, or caps, for each of FY2012-FY2021. If Congress appropriates more than allowed under these limits in any given year, sequestration would cancel the excess amount.

- Failure of Congress to enact legislation developed by a Joint Select Committee on Deficit Reduction, by January 15, 2012, to reduce the deficit by at least $1.2 trillion. The BCA provided that such failure would trigger a series of automatic spending reductions, including sequestration of mandatory spending in each of FY2013-FY2021, a one-year sequestration of discretionary spending for FY2013, and lower discretionary spending limits for each of FY2014-FY2021.

In fact, the Joint Committee did not develop the necessary legislation and Congress did not meet the January 15, 2012, deadline. Thus, the first automatic spending cuts under the BCA are now scheduled to take effect on January 2, 2013. Pursuant to the Sequestration Transparency Act (P.L. 112-155), the Administration issued a report on September 14 that previews the estimated impact of that sequestration on discretionary and mandatory spending.

Under the Statutory PAYGO Act, sequestration is part of a budget enforcement mechanism that is intended to prevent enactment of mandatory spending and revenue legislation that would increase the federal deficit. This act requires the Office of Management and Budget (OMB) to track costs and savings associated with enacted legislation and to determine at the end of each congressional session if net total costs exceed net total savings. If so, a sequestration will be triggered.

If sequestration is triggered—either under the BCA or Statutory PAYGO Act—the exemptions and special rules of Sections 255 and 256 of BBEDCA apply. Most exempt programs are mandatory, and include Social Security and Medicaid; refundable tax credits to individuals; and low-income programs such as the Children's Health Insurance Program, Supplemental Nutrition Assistance Program, Temporary Assistance for Needy Families, and Supplemental Security Income. Some discretionary programs also are exempt, notably all programs administered by the Department of Veterans Affairs. Also, subject to notification of Congress by the President, military personnel accounts may either be exempt or reduced by a lower percentage.

Special rules also apply to several, primarily mandatory, programs. For example, under Section 256 of BBEDCA, Medicare may not be sequestered by more than 4%. However, under a sequester triggered by the BCA, reduction of Medicare is further limited to no more than 2%.

Contents

Tables

Appendixes

Contacts

Introduction

"Sequestration" is a process of automatic, largely across-the-board spending reductions to meet or enforce certain budget policy goals.[1] It was first established by the Balanced Budget and Emergency Deficit Control Act of 1985 (BBEDCA, Title II of P.L. 99-177, 2 U.S.C. 900-922) to enforce deficit targets. In the 1990s, sequestration was used to enforce statutory limits on discretionary spending and a pay-as-you-go (PAYGO) requirement on direct spending and revenue legislation. After effectively expiring in 2002, sequestration was reestablished by the Statutory Pay-As-You-Go Act of 2010 (P.L. 111-139) to enforce a modified PAYGO requirement on direct spending and revenue legislation. Most recently, under the Budget Control Act of 2011 (BCA, P.L. 112-25), sequestration was tied to enforcement of new statutory limits on discretionary spending and achievement of the budget goal established for the Joint Select Committee on Deficit Reduction. Under current law, a sequestration has been triggered by the BCA and is scheduled to occur on January 2, 2013, to affect spending for FY2013.

In general, sequestration entails the permanent cancellation of budgetary resources by a uniform percentage.[2] Moreover, this uniform percentage reduction is applied to all programs, projects, and activities within a budget account.[3] However, the current sequestration procedures, as in previous iterations of such procedures, provide for exemptions and special rules. That is, certain programs and activities are exempt from sequestration, and certain other programs are governed by special rules regarding the application of a sequester. This report provides an overview of those exemptions and special rules, which are generally found in Sections 255 and 256 of BBEDCA, as amended (2 U.S.C. 905 and 906).

Current Sequestration Triggers

As noted above, sequestration is tied to certain budget goals established in the Budget Control Act of 2011, as well as in the Statutory PAYGO Act of 2010. To provide some context for the exemptions and special rules applicable to these sequestration procedures, brief descriptions of the budget goals that may be enforced by sequestration are provided below. For more detailed information on current budget constraints and goals, readers should consult CRS Report R41965, *The Budget Control Act of 2011*, by Bill Heniff Jr., Elizabeth Rybicki, and Shannon M. Mahan; and CRS Report R41157, *The Statutory Pay-As-You-Go Act of 2010: Summary and Legislative History*, by Bill Heniff Jr. For analysis of the impact of BCA, see CRS Report R42506, *The Budget Control Act of 2011: The Effects on Spending and the Budget Deficit When the Automatic Spending Cuts Are Implemented*, by Mindy R. Levit and Marc Labonte, and CRS Report R42675, *The Budget Control Act of 2011: Budgetary Effects of Proposals to Replace the FY2013 Sequester*, by Mindy R. Levit.

---

[1] For more information on sequestration and its historical application, see (1) CRS Report RL31137, *Sequestration Procedures Under the 1985 Balanced Budget Act*, by Robert Keith; (2) CRS Report RS20398, *Budget Sequesters: A Brief Review*, by Robert Keith; and (3) CRS Report R41901, *Statutory Budget Controls in Effect Between 1985 and 2002*, by Megan Suzanne Lynch.

[2] "Budgetary resources" include new budget authority, unobligated balances, direct spending authority, and obligation limitations, as defined in Section 250(c)(6) of the BBEDCA, as amended.

[3] For accounts included in appropriations acts, "programs, projects, and activities" (PPAs) within each budget account are delineated in those acts or accompanying reports; and for accounts not included in appropriations acts, they are delineated in the most recently submitted President's budget.

Sequestration Triggers Under the BCA

The Budget Control Act of 2011 (BCA) was enacted on August 2, 2011. It provided for increases in the debt limit and established procedures designed to reduce the federal budget deficit.[4] As enacted, the BCA had two primary components that could trigger a sequestration of discretionary and/or mandatory (or direct) spending:[5]

- Title I of the BCA established discretionary spending limits, or caps, for each of FY2012-FY2021.[6] If Congress appropriated more than allowed under these spending limits in any given year, the automatic reduction process of sequestration would cancel the excess amount. For FY2012 and FY2013, the spending limits were divided into "security" and "nonsecurity" categories, with security defined broadly to include the Departments of Veterans Affairs (VA), Homeland Security (DHS), and State, in addition to the Department of Defense and certain other activities.[7] For FY2014 and subsequent years, no distinction was made between security and nonsecurity, and Title I of the law established a single discretionary spending limit for each year.

- Title IV of the BCA established a bipartisan Joint Select Committee on Deficit Reduction. Failure by Congress to enact legislation by January 15, 2012, developed by the Joint Committee and reducing the deficit by at least $1.2 trillion, would trigger a series of automatic spending reductions intended to achieve that level of savings over the FY2013-FY2021 period. These automatic reductions include sequestration of mandatory spending for each of FY2013-FY2021, a one-year sequestration of discretionary spending for FY2013, and lower discretionary spending limits for FY2014-FY2021. Spending reductions would be divided equally between security and nonsecurity. However, *these terms are redefined*, so that "security" consists only of budget function 050 (effectively, the Department of Defense), and "nonsecurity" includes all other government spending (including the VA, DHS, and State). The distinction between security and nonsecurity (*as redefined*) remains for each of FY2014-FY2021.

The security-nonsecurity distinction is significant because sequestration is imposed within these categories. In other words, if Congress appropriated more than allowed for either category in a given year, the excess spending would be canceled in the category where the breach occurred. As noted above, security was defined broadly under Title I, and spending was divided between the

---

[4] For a comprehensive discussion of the BCA, see CRS Report R41965, *The Budget Control Act of 2011*, by Bill Heniff Jr., Elizabeth Rybicki, and Shannon M. Mahan.

[5] Discretionary spending is provided in and controlled through the annual appropriations process and represents a portion of total federal spending. The other portion, referred to as direct spending (or mandatory spending), is generally provided in or controlled by authorizing legislation that requires federal payments to individuals or entities, often based on eligibility criteria and benefit formulas set forth in statute. Some direct spending is funded in appropriations acts, referred to as appropriated entitlements, but is controlled by the authorizing statute(s).

[6] Adjustments are allowed to these discretionary spending limits for certain specified activities, such as costs associated with disability redeterminations, health care fraud and abuse, overseas contingency operations and the War on Terror, emergency spending, and funding for disasters.

[7] The Office of Management and Budget (OMB) has determined that discretionary amounts provided for FY2012 were within the BCA spending limits, so that no sequestration was necessary for that year. See http://www.whitehouse.gov/sites/default/files/omb/assets/legislative_reports/sequestration/sequestration_final_jan2012.pdf.

---

two categories only for two years; a single discretionary spending limit was set for FY2014 and subsequent years. However, under the automatic procedures triggered by failure of the Joint Committee, security is defined more narrowly and the separate security and nonsecurity categories remain in effect for each year through FY2021.

Because the Joint Committee did not, in fact, develop legislation to achieve the specified level of deficit reduction ($1.2 trillion) by the deadline set in the BCA, and Congress did not subsequently enact such legislation by January 15, 2012, the automatic budget enforcement procedures provided by the law are now scheduled to occur.[8] The first fiscal year these procedures will affect is FY2013; sequestration of excess spending for that fiscal year (as outlined in the second bullet on the previous page) is scheduled to happen on January 2, 2013.

The automatic procedures triggered by failure of the Joint Committee process will affect both mandatory and discretionary spending, and will result in the security and nonsecurity categories being reduced by an equal amount of spending in each of FY2013 through FY2021. Because the definition of "security" is revised to mean primarily the Department of Defense, this means that half of the necessary spending reductions will come from that department while the other half will come from the rest of the federal budget.[9]

OMB's Preliminary Estimates of the January 2013 Sequester

On August 7, President Obama signed into law the Sequestration Transparency Act (P.L. 112-155), which required the Administration to report to Congress within 30 days of enactment on the impact of the January 2, 2013, sequestration. In this report, the President was to identify all accounts to be sequestered—discretionary and mandatory, defense and nondefense—and estimate the sequestration percentages to be applied and the amounts necessary to achieve the required savings. Accounts were to be identified at the "program, project and activity" (PPA) level (see footnote 3). For discretionary accounts funded through enacted FY2013 appropriations laws, estimates were to be based on those funding levels; for other discretionary accounts, estimates were to be based on an assumed continuing resolution at FY2012 levels. Estimates for mandatory accounts were to be based on estimated spending under current law. The law further required the President to identify all exempt discretionary and mandatory accounts, and to include any other data or information that would help the public understand the impact of sequestration.

The President's Office of Management and Budget (OMB) issued the report required by P.L. 112-155 on September 14, noting that its estimates and classifications of whether a program is exempt or subject to sequestration are "preliminary."[10] "If the sequestration were to occur, the actual results would differ based on changes in law and ongoing legal, budgetary, and technical analysis," according to OMB. For example, the Sequestration Transparency Act directed OMB to

---

[8] For the statement of the Joint Committee co-chairs, announcing they would not meet the statutory deadline, see http://www.murray.senate.gov/public/index.cfm/2011/11/statement-from-co-chairs-of-the-joint-select-committee-on-deficit-reduction.

[9] For the mechanics of the BCA's automatic spending reduction procedures, see the section titled "Budget Goal Enforcement: Spending Reduction Trigger" in CRS Report R41965, *The Budget Control Act of 2011*, by Bill Heniff Jr., Elizabeth Rybicki, and Shannon M. Mahan. Also see Congressional Budget Office, *Estimated Impact of Automatic Budget Enforcement Procedures Specified in the Budget Control Act*, http://www.cbo.gov/publication/42754.

[10] *OMB Report Pursuant to the Sequestration Transparency Act of 2012 (P.L. 112-155)*, September 2012, available at http://www.whitehouse.gov/sites/default/files/omb/assets/legislative_reports/stareport.pdf. Hereinafter referred to as *OMB Report Pursuant to the Sequestration Transparency Act*, September 2012.

base its estimates on the assumption that a continuing resolution would be enacted for FY2013 that would maintain discretionary spending at FY2012 levels. Following enactment of P.L. 112-155, however, Congress enacted a continuing resolution for the first six months of FY2013 (P.L. 112-175) that will maintain funding at FY2012 levels, *plus* an additional 0.612%. Moreover, while OMB provided estimates of the percentage reductions that would occur under sequestration at the account level, it did not provide that information for each PPA, stating that "additional time is necessary to identify, review, and resolve issues associated with providing information at this level of detail."

Subject to numerous caveats presented in the report, OMB's preliminary estimates of the percentage reductions that will occur under the BCA-triggered sequester scheduled for January 2013 are shown in **Table 1**.

Table I. Preliminary OMB Estimates of FY2013 Uniform Percent Reductions Under BCA-Triggered Sequester Scheduled for January 2, 2013

Category of Funding	Defense	Nondefense
Nonexempt Discretionary	9.4%	8.2%
Nonexempt Mandatory (other than Medicare and selected health programs)	10.0%	7.6%
Medicare and mandatory components of selected health programs	na	2.0%

Source: OMB Report Pursuant to the Sequestration Transparency Act of 2012 (P.L. 112-155), September 2012.

Notes: "Defense" and "Nondefense" are the same as the *revised* Security and Nonsecurity categories discussed above, where Defense (or revised Security) equals budget function 050, and Nondefense (or revised Nonsecurity) equals everything else. Estimates shown are preliminary and will change if sequestration occurs in January 2013. See pp. 1-10 of the OMB report for a full discussion of the limitations of these estimates. na = not applicable. See sections, later in this CRS report, headed "Section 255 Program Exemptions" and "Section 256 Special Rules" for discussion of exemptions and special rules, including those applicable to Medicare and selected health programs.

Sequestration Trigger Under Statutory PAYGO

The Statutory Pay-As-You-Go Act of 2010 was enacted on February 12, 2010, as Title I of P.L. 111-139.[11] It established a permanent budget enforcement mechanism intended to prevent mandatory (i.e., direct) spending and revenue legislation that would increase the deficit from being passed and signed into law. (Statutory PAYGO does not apply to discretionary spending.) The act requires various scorekeeping procedures, including five-year and 10-year scorecards that track costs and savings associated with enacted legislation. At the end of each congressional session, OMB generally must determine whether the net effect of direct spending and revenue legislation enacted during the session has increased the deficit, and if so, a sequestration will be triggered.

---

[11] For a detailed discussion of the Statutory PAYGO Act, see CRS Report R41157, *The Statutory Pay-As-You-Go Act of 2010: Summary and Legislative History*, by Bill Heniff Jr.

Certain costs and savings are not counted toward Statutory PAYGO, including designated emergency spending, debt service costs, costs associated with a shift in timing of certain outlays, and net savings from the CLASS Act.[12] In addition, the law provided that if enacted by December 31, 2011, costs associated with four specified categories of legislation (Medicare physicians' payments, the estate and gift tax, the alternative minimum tax, and certain "middle-class" tax cuts) would be excluded within limits set forth in the act. This provision has not been extended to apply to legislation enacted after 2011.

Program Exemptions and Special Rules for Sequestration

Certain programs are exempt from sequestration, and special rules govern the sequestration of others. For the most part, these provisions are found in Sections 255 and 256 of the Balanced Budget and Emergency Deficit Control Act (BBEDCA), as amended. These provisions would apply to sequestration orders that occur under either the BCA or the Statutory PAYGO Act. However, the application of these rules for certain programs might differ, depending on the specific provision that triggers the sequestration.

Questions about the impact of sequestration on any particular program or account cannot be answered strictly from reading the relevant provisions of law. If sequestration occurs, all nonexempt "programs, projects, and activities" must be reduced by a uniform percentage (unless provided otherwise under special rules; see "Section 256 Special Rules"). However, numerous factors potentially affect the sequestration process, including the amount of budgetary resources subject to sequestration and the interpretation of statutory requirements as they apply to specific programs and activities.

Section 255 of BBEDCA (codified at 2 U.S.C. 905) identifies programs that are exempt from sequestration, and Section 256 of BBEDCA (codified at 2 U.S.C. 906) establishes special rules. Readers should note that these sections have been amended as recently as February 2010, under the Statutory PAYGO Act; however, an actual sequestration has not occurred since the early 1990s.[13] Thus, CRS cannot say with certainty how these provisions may be interpreted and applied in a future sequestration, including the sequestration scheduled to occur in January 2013, or how potential ambiguities in language may be resolved. The following should be considered as only a general description of the law and not an attempted interpretation. Ultimately, the execution and impact of any automatic spending reduction triggered under provisions of the BCA or Statutory PAYGO will depend in large part on the legal interpretations and actions taken by OMB. As discussed earlier, OMB issued a report in September 2012, pursuant to the Sequestration Transparency Act (P.L. 112-155), which estimates the potential impact of the BCA sequester slated for January 2013. That report provides preliminary insight into OMB's likely interpretation of specific provisions if the sequestration occurs as scheduled.

---

[12] The CLASS Act was anticipated but not yet enacted at the time P.L. 111-139 was enacted. See CRS Report R40842, *Community Living Assistance Services and Supports (CLASS) Provisions in the Patient Protection and Affordable Care Act (ACA)*, by Janemarie Mulvey and Kirsten J. Colello.

[13] See CRS Report RS20398, *Budget Sequesters: A Brief Review*, by Robert Keith, dated March 8, 2004.

Section 255 Program Exemptions[14]

Section 255 contains a list of programs and activities that are exempt from sequestration.[15] Most are mandatory, although a few are discretionary, most notably programs administered by the Department of Veterans Affairs (VA). In many cases, specific budget accounts are provided, so readers are referred to the statute for precise identification of exempted programs and activities (see **Appendix**). While the law provides a list of programs and types of spending that are exempt from sequestration, it provides no definitive list of programs or types of spending that would absolutely *be* subject to sequestration. As stated above, the impact of sequestration on any given program will depend on the actions and interpretations of OMB. The following are selected programs and types of spending identified in Section 255 as exempt from sequestration; readers are referred to the report issued by OMB in September 2012, pursuant to the Sequestration Transparency Act, for a preliminary look at how OMB might interpret these provisions with regard to individual accounts in implementing the sequestration scheduled for January 2013:

- Social Security benefits (old-age, survivors, and disability) and Tier 1 Railroad Retirement benefits.

- All programs administered by the VA, and special benefits for certain World War II veterans.[16]

- Net interest (budget function 900).

- Payments to individuals in the form of refundable tax credits.[17]

- Unobligated balances, carried over from prior years, for nondefense programs.

- At the President's discretion (subject to notification to Congress), military personnel accounts may be exempt entirely, or a lower sequestration percentage may apply.[18]

- A list of "other" budget accounts and activities; readers should consult the statute for a complete list. A few selected examples include

    - activities resulting from private donations, bequests or voluntary contributions, or financed by voluntary payments for good or services;

---

[14] See **Appendix** for the complete statutory language of Section 255 of BBEDCA.

[15] For a table showing some of the largest programs exempt from sequestration, including their FY2010 budgetary authority and discretionary/mandatory status, see Table 4 in CRS Report R42013, *The Budget Control Act of 2011: How Do the Discretionary Caps and Automatic Spending Cuts Affect the Budget and the Economy?*, by Marc Labonte and Mindy R. Levit.

[16] In its report issued pursuant to the Sequestration Transparency Act, OMB clarified that the exemption for VA programs would also apply to the agency's administrative expenses. Also, see discussion of special rules in the "Veterans' Medical Care" section, below.

[17] These would include the Earned Income Tax Credit and the refundable portion of the Child Tax Credit (sometimes referred to as the Additional Child Tax Credit.). In addition, the Patient Protection and Affordable Care Act (ACA, P.L. 111-148, as amended) established a refundable tax credit for individuals and families with incomes between specified levels to help them purchase health insurance coverage; presumably this tax credit also would be exempt. See CRS Report R42051, *Budget Control Act: Potential Impact of Sequestration on Health Reform Spending*, by C. Stephen Redhead.

[18] On July 31, 2012, Acting OMB Director Jeffrey Zients notified Congress of the President's intent to exempt military personnel accounts from sequestration: http://www.whitehouse.gov/sites/default/files/omb/legislative/letters/military-personnel-letter-biden.pdf.

- advances to the Unemployment Trust Fund;[19]
- payments to various retirement, health care, and disability trust funds;
- certain Tribal and Indian trust accounts; and
- Medical Facilities Guaranty and Loan Fund.

- Specified federal retirement and disability accounts and activities (consult the statute for the complete list).

- Prior legal obligations of the federal government in specified budget accounts (consult the statute for the complete list).[20]

- Low-income programs, including

  - Academic Competitiveness/Smart Grant Program;[21]

  - mandatory funding under the Child Care and Development Fund;

  - Child Nutrition Programs (including School Lunch, School Breakfast, Child and Adult Care Food, and others, but excluding Special Milk);

  - Children's Health Insurance Program (CHIP);

  - Commodity Supplemental Food Program;

  - Temporary Assistance for Needy Families (TANF) and the TANF Contingency Fund;

  - Family Support Programs;[22]

  - Federal Pell Grants;

  - Medicaid;

  - Foster Care and Permanency Programs;

  - Supplemental Nutrition Assistance Program (SNAP, formerly food stamps); and

  - Supplemental Security Income (SSI).

- Medicare Part D low-income premium and cost-sharing subsidies; Medicare Part D catastrophic subsidy payments; and Qualified Individual (QI) premiums.[23]

- Specified economic recovery programs, including GSE Preferred Stock Purchase Agreements, the Office of Financial Stability, and the Special Inspector General for the Troubled Asset Relief Program.

---

[19] Also see discussion of special rules in the "Unemployment Compensation" section, below.

[20] Programs on the list include the Federal Crop Insurance Corporation Fund; the exemption of prior legal obligations for agriculture is similar to a special rule under Section 256 of BBEDCA for the Commodity Credit Corporation (discussed below).

[21] Due to sunset provisions, no grants can be made under this program after June 30, 2011.

[22] This account includes the Child Support Enforcement program. See discussion of special rules in the "Child Support Enforcement" section, below.

[23] These programs are not listed in Section 255, but instead Section 256(d) identifies them as programs exempt from sequestration "in addition to" the programs listed in Section 255. See the "Medicare" section, below.

- The following "split-treatment" programs, to the extent that the programs' budgetary resources are subject to obligations limitations in appropriations bills:
  - Federal Aid-Highways;
  - Highway Traffic Safety Grants;
  - Operations and Research NHTSA and National Driver Register;
  - Motor Carrier Safety Operations and Programs;
  - Motor Carrier Safety Grants;
  - Formula and Bus Grants; and
  - Grants-in-Aid for Airports.

Section 256 Special Rules

In addition to the exemptions in Section 255 of BBEDCA, Section 256 establishes special rules for sequestration of certain programs or types of spending. Most Section 256 special rules apply to mandatory programs, although some discretionary programs are included (e.g., certain health programs). Once again, the effect of sequestration on any given program is subject to the interpretation of the law's provisions by OMB.

The following is a list of programs included in Section 256 (they are discussed in greater detail below):

- student loans under Title IV-B and IV-D of the Higher Education Act;
- Medicare;
- community and migrant health centers, Indian health services and facilities, and veterans' medical care;
- Child Support Enforcement;
- federal pay;
- federal administrative expenses;
- Unemployment Compensation; and
- Commodity Credit Corporation.

Student Loans[24]

Special sequestration rules (Section 256(b)) apply to federal student loans made under the William D. Ford Federal Direct Loan (DL) program during the period when a sequestration order is in effect. Origination fees on DL program loans made during a period of sequestration must be increased by the uniform percentage specified in the sequestration order.[25] Loan origination fees

---

[24] This section was prepared by David Smole, dsmole@crs.loc.gov, 7-0624.

[25] Sections 251A(8) and 256(b) of BBEDCA. The William D. Ford Federal Direct Loan (DL) program is authorized under Title IV, Part D of the Higher Education Act of 1965 (HEA), as amended. BBEDCA, §256(b) references federal (continued...)

are calculated as a proportion of the loan principal borrowed and are deducted proportionately from each disbursement of the loan proceeds to the borrower. The origination fee helps offset the costs of federal loan subsidies.

Four types of federal student loans are made under the DL program: Subsidized Stafford Loans, Unsubsidized Stafford Loans, PLUS Loans, and Consolidation Loans.[26] In general, for DL program loans made on or after July 1, 2010, the origination fee on Subsidized Stafford Loans and Unsubsidized Stafford loans is 1%, and the origination fee on PLUS Loans is 4%. The Department of Education does not currently charge an origination fee on Consolidation Loans.

Under a sequestration order applicable to direct spending programs, origination fees on DL program loans made during the sequestration period would be required to be increased by the uniform percentage amount. As illustrated in **Table 1**, OMB estimates a uniform percentage amount of 7.6% for nonexempt nondefense mandatory programs. Thus, the 1% origination fee on Subsidized Stafford Loans and Unsubsidized Stafford Loans and the 4% origination fee on PLUS loans would each be increased by 7.6% (i.e., the estimated uniform percentage factor).

Medicare[27]

Enacted in 1965, the Medicare program provides hospital and supplementary medical insurance to Americans age 65 and older and to disabled persons, including those with end-stage renal disease. Medicare enrollment has increased from 19 million in 1966 to about 50 million beneficiaries in FY2012. CBO estimates that by 2022, the number of Medicare enrollees will increase by about a third, to almost 67 million.[28]

Medicare consists of two parts financed through separate trust funds. Hospital Insurance (Part A) pays health care providers for inpatient care that beneficiaries receive at hospitals; it also pays for care at skilled nursing facilities, some home health care, and hospice services. Supplementary Medical Insurance (Parts B and D) pays for physicians' services, outpatient services at hospitals, home health care, and outpatient prescription drugs. (Payments to private insurance plans under Part C are financed by a blend of funds from the two trust funds.) Medicare is administered by the Centers for Medicare & Medicaid Services (CMS), within the Department of Health and Human Services (HHS).

CBO estimates that in FY2012 gross Medicare outlays will total $575.7 billion.[29] Most of this spending (about 99%) is comprised of mandatory spending that is primarily used to cover benefit

---

(...continued)

student loans made under HEA, Title IV, Part B and Part D, during the period when a sequestration order is in effect. With the enactment of the SAFRA Act, part of the Health Care and Education Reconciliation Act of 2010 (HCERA; P.L. 111-152), student loans are no longer being made under HEA, Title IV, Part B (the Federal Family Education Loan (FFEL) program). As such, the special rule applies only to student loans made under HEA, Title IV, Part D (i.e., DL program loans).

[26] For additional information on DL program loans, see CRS Report R40122, *Federal Student Loans Made Under the Federal Family Education Loan Program and the William D. Ford Federal Direct Loan Program: Terms and Conditions for Borrowers*, by David P. Smole.

[27] This section was prepared by Patricia Davis, pdavis@crs.loc.gov, 7-7362.

[28] Congressional Budget Office, March 2012 Medicare Baseline, http://www.cbo.gov/sites/default/files/cbofiles/attachments/43060_Medicare.pdf

[29] Congressional Budget Office, March 2012 Medicare Baseline, http://www.cbo.gov/sites/default/files/cbofiles/
(continued...)

---

payments (i.e., payments to health care providers for their services). CBO projects that spending on Medicare benefits will increase from $555.9 billion in FY2012 to about $1 trillion in FY2022,[30] an annual growth rate of 7%.

About 0.5% of Medicare mandatory outlays are used for administrative purposes, such as funding quality improvement organizations, certain activities against fraud and abuse, and payments of Part B premiums for Qualifying Individuals.[31] A small portion of Medicare spending is discretionary (about $6.3 billion in FY2012). This portion is used almost entirely for program management activities, such as payments to contractors to process providers' claims, funding for beneficiary outreach and education, and the maintenance of Medicare's information technology (IT) infrastructure.

Sequestration Rules for Medicare

Section 256(d) of BBEDCA contains special rules for the Medicare program in case of a sequestration. However, while BBEDCA ordinarily limits reduction of certain Medicare spending to 4% under a sequestration order (which would apply in the case of a Statutory PAYGO sequestration), the BCA limits the size of this reduction to 2%.

As stated earlier, if sequestration occurs all nonexempt programs must be reduced by a uniform percentage. This percentage is calculated by OMB, based on the necessary amount of spending reduction that must occur overall. Under a sequestration triggered by the BCA, if the uniform percentage is less than 2%, it will be applied to all nonexempt accounts, including Medicare. If the percentage is greater than 2%, then a 2% reduction will be made in Medicare spending, and the uniform reduction percentage for the remaining programs will be recalculated and increased by the amount necessary to achieve the total level of reductions needed. If sequestration were triggered by Statutory PAYGO, the process would be the same but Medicare sequestration would be limited to 4%.

Under sequestration, Medicare's benefit structure would generally remain unchanged (i.e., beneficiaries would not see a change in their Medicare coverage). Additionally, spending for certain Medicare programs and activities are exempt from sequestration and would therefore not be reduced under a sequestration order. These include (1) Part D low-income subsidies;[32] (2) the Part D catastrophic subsidy; and (3) Qualified Individual (QI) premiums.[33]

(...continued)

attachments/43060_Medicare.pdf

[30] Congressional Budget Office, March 2012 Medicare Baseline, http://www.cbo.gov/sites/default/files/cbofiles/attachments/43060_Medicare.pdf

[31] The Qualifying Individual Program (QI) is one of the Medicare Savings Programs and covers the Part B premium for eligible individuals. To be eligible for the QI program, one must be entitled to Medicare Part A, have an income of at least 120% of the Federal Poverty Level (FPL) but less than 135% of FPL with resources not exceeding twice the limit for SSI eligibility, and not be otherwise eligible for Medicaid benefits. Mandatory funding is provided through 2012.

[32] See CRS Report R40425, *Medicare Primer*, coordinated by Patricia A. Davis for an overview of the Medicare Part D benefit.

[33] The report issued by OMB in September 2012, pursuant to the Sequestration Transparency Act, specified that certain additional Medicare-related funds would also be exempt from sequestration under Section 225(g)(1)(A) of BBEDCA. Mandatory spending for Quality Improvement Organizations and discretionary spending for the Office of Medicare Hearings and Appeals would be exempt as intragovernmental payments; and mandatory payments to health care trust funds are specifically listed as exempt in Section 225(g)(1)(A).

For payments made under Medicare Parts A and B, the percentage reductions are to be made to individual payments to providers for services (e.g., hospital and physician services). In the case of Parts C and D, reductions are to be made to the monthly payments to the private plans that administer these parts of Medicare. Reductions are to be made at a uniform rate and are not to exceed 2%. In the case of inpatient services, the services are considered to be furnished on the date of the individual's discharge from the inpatient facility. For services paid on a reasonable cost basis,[34] the reduction is to be applied to payments for such services incurred at any time during each cost reporting period during the sequestration period, for the portion of the cost reporting period that occurs during the effective period of the order. For Part B services provided under assignment,[35] the reduced payment would be considered *payment in full* and the Medicare beneficiary would not pay higher copayments to make up for the reduced amount. CBO estimates that Medicare benefit spending will be reduced by about $99.3 billion over the nine-year sequestration period.[36]

Section 256(d) of the BBEDCA specifies that the Secretary may not take into account any reductions in payment amounts under sequestration for purposes of computing any adjustments to Medicare payment rates, including the Part C growth percentage, the Part D annual growth rate, and the determination of Medicare Part D risk corridors.[37] In other words, annual provider and plan payment updates may be determined as if the reductions under sequestration had not taken place.

Special Considerations Regarding Medicare

The budgetary baseline that must be used in implementing a sequestration has special implications with regard to Medicare. For direct spending, the baseline is to be calculated by assuming that the laws providing or creating direct spending will operate in the manner specified, and that funding for entitlement authority is adequate to make all required payments.[38]

Specifically, CBO's projections of Medicare spending incorporate the assumption that Medicare spending will be constrained beginning in 2013 by the sustainable growth rate (SGR) mechanism used to calculate the fees paid for physicians' services.[39] Under current law, those fees will be reduced by about 27% beginning in January 2013 and by additional amounts in subsequent years. If future legislation overrides the scheduled reductions, as has happened every year since 2003, then spending for Medicare will be greater than the amounts projected in the baseline. CBO

---

[34] Most providers are paid under a prospective payment system or fee schedule. Some types of providers, such as Critical Access Hospitals, are paid on a reasonable cost basis under which payments are based on actual costs incurred. Reasonable cost is defined at Social Security Act §1861(v).

[35] Assignment is an agreement by a doctor, provider, or supplier to be paid directly by Medicare, to accept the payment amount Medicare approves for the service, and not to bill the beneficiary for any more than the Medicare deductible and coinsurance (if applicable). Providers that don't accept assignment may charge more than the Medicare-approved amount.

[36] Congressional Budget Office, March 2012 Medicare Baseline, http://www.cbo.gov/sites/default/files/cbofiles/attachments/43060_Medicare.pdf

[37] Information on Medicare provider payments and the determination of updates may be found in CRS Report RL30526, *Medicare Payment Updates and Payment Rates*, coordinated by Paulette C. Morgan.

[38] BBEDCA §257(b)(1).

[39] See CRS Report R40907, *Medicare Physician Payment Updates and the Sustainable Growth Rate (SGR) System*, by Jim Hahn and Janemarie Mulvey.

estimated a 10-year cost of freezing payments at current levels at close to $300 billion for 2012-2021; if payments were increased by a medical inflation factor, the cost could be even higher.[40]

It is also unclear how reductions under sequestration will affect or be affected by the operations of the Independent Payment Advisory Board (IPAB).[41] The IPAB, established by the Patient Protection and Affordable Care Act (ACA, P.L. 111-148), is responsible for restraining the growth rate of Medicare spending per enrollee. If the growth of such spending is projected to exceed specified targets, the IPAB is required to submit proposals to reduce it, and the Secretary must implement these proposals unless the Congress acts to change them. While CBO's baseline projections incorporate estimates of potential savings from the IPAB process, it remains to be determined (1) whether the target growth rate would be calculated using the expected rate outside of sequestration or under sequestration; (2) whether IPAB would be able to find and recommend additional savings on top of the sequestered amounts; and (3) how savings associated with future reductions under IPAB would factor into the baseline used to determine needed reductions under sequestration.

There have also been some concerns that although Medicare benefits are not to be reduced under sequestration, reductions in provider payments, in addition to reductions already mandated under ACA,[42] could discourage some providers from accepting Medicare patients. For instance, the Medicare Trustees have cautioned that reductions to certain providers under ACA may not be sustainable over the long term,[43] and the Office of the Actuary for CMS has provided alternative projections assuming that these reductions are gradually phased out beginning in 2020.[44] Additionally, there is concern that costs could be shifted to other third-party payers or beneficiaries to make up for the additional decrease in payments. For instance, private payers could see increased costs or Medicare Advantage or Prescription Drug Sponsors could design their plans in future years so that Medicare enrollees pay higher premiums and/or increased cost sharing.

Further, while Section 257 of the BBEDCA specifies that "the receipts and disbursements of the Hospital Insurance Trust Fund shall be included in all calculations," it does not address how beneficiary Part B premiums would be determined under sequestration. As Part B premiums are based on a percentage of expected Part B spending and such spending would be lower under sequestration, it remains to be determined whether premiums would be adjusted downward to reflect these lower expected costs.

---

[40] Congressional Budget Office, *Medicare's Payments to Physicians: The Budgetary Impact of Alternative Policies*, June 16, 2011, http://www.cbo.gov/ftpdocs/122xx/doc12240/SGR_Menu_2011.pdf.

[41] See CRS Report R41511, *The Independent Payment Advisory Board*, by Jim Hahn and Christopher M. Davis.

[42] See CRS Report R41196, *Medicare Provisions in the Patient Protection and Affordable Care Act (PPACA): Summary and Timeline*, coordinated by Patricia A. Davis.

[43] Statement of Actuarial Opinion of the 2012 Annual Report of the Boards of Trustees of the Federal Hospital Insurance and Federal Supplementary Medical Insurance Trust Funds, https://www.cms.gov/Research-Statistics-Data-and-Systems/Statistics-Trends-and-Reports/ReportsTrustFunds/downloads//tr2012.pdf.

[44] 2012 Annual Report of the Boards of Trustees of the Federal Hospital Insurance and Federal Supplementary Medical Insurance Trust Funds, Appendix C, https://www.cms.gov/Research-Statistics-Data-and-Systems/Statistics-Trends-and-Reports/ReportsTrustFunds/downloads//tr2012.pdf.

Health Centers, Indian Health, and Veterans' Medical Care

Health Centers[45]

Community and migrant health centers are two types of federally funded health centers: nonprofit entities that receive grants to provide primary care to people who experience financial, geographic, cultural, or other barriers to health care. They are administered by the Health Resources and Services Administration (HRSA) within the Department of Health and Human Services (HHS). In addition to these two types of health centers, HRSA provides grants to support health centers for the homeless and health centers for residents of public housing.

Section 256(e) of BBEDCA limits the amount of funding that can be reduced from community and migrant health centers under a sequestration to 2%. At the time of BBEDCA's enactment in 1985, there were four separate health center programs administered by HRSA and funded under HRSA's budget account. The Health Centers Consolidation Act of 1996 (P.L. 104-299) combined the four health center programs—community health centers, migrant health centers, health centers for the homeless, and health centers for residents of public housing—into Section 330 of the Public Health Service Act, which receives a single discretionary appropriation as part of the HRSA budget. With regard to the sequester scheduled to take place on January 2, 2013, however, OMB has determined that this special rule for community and migrant health centers applies only to mandatory funds and not to discretionary funds.[46] Given this determination, the 2% limit applies to mandatory appropriations that the health center program received under the Patient Protection and Affordable Care Act (ACA, P.L. 111-148), from FY2011 through FY2015.[47]

Indian Health Service[48]

The Indian Health Service (IHS) in HHS is responsible for providing comprehensive medical and environmental health services for approximately 1.9 million American Indians and Alaska Natives who belong to 565 federally recognized tribes located in 35 states. Health care is provided through a system of facilities and programs operated by IHS, tribes and tribal groups, and urban Indian organizations. IHS is funded by two discretionary budget accounts—Indian Health Services and Indian Health Facilities. However, IHS also receives reimbursements from Medicare, Medicaid, and the Children's Health Insurance Program (CHIP) for services provided at IHS facilities for beneficiaries eligible for these programs, and in FY2012 and FY2013, IHS will receive mandatory appropriations for diabetes programs.[49]

Under Section 256(e) of BBEDCA, sequestration may only reduce funding for the two IHS accounts by 2% in any fiscal year. With regard to the sequester scheduled to take place on January 2, 2013, however, OMB has determined that this special rule (i.e., the 2% limit) will only apply to mandatory funds that IHS receives (i.e., diabetes program funding). The IHS discretionary

---

[45] This section was prepared by Elayne Heisler, eheisler@crs.loc.gov, 7-4453.

[46] See discussion on pp. 4-5 of *OMB Report Pursuant to the Sequestration Transparency Act*, September 2012.

[47] See CRS Report R41301, *Appropriations and Fund Transfers in the Patient Protection and Affordable Care Act (PPACA)*, by C. Stephen Redhead.

[48] This section was prepared by Elayne Heisler, eheisler@crs.loc.gov, 7-4453.

[49] Appropriated under P.L. 111-309.

appropriation thus would be fully sequesterable at OMB's estimated rate of 8.2%.[50] OMB did not include reimbursements that IHS receives from other federal programs, or rent that IHS receives from renting staff quarters in the amount that could be sequestered from the IHS budget (i.e., it exempted these amounts from sequestration).

Veterans' Medical Care[51]

The VA, through the Veterans Health Administration (VHA), operates the nation's largest integrated direct health care delivery system.[52] Veterans' medical care is a discretionary program, and eligibility for VA medical care is based on veteran status, presence of service-connected disabilities or exposures, income, and/or other factors, such as status as a former prisoner of war or receipt of a Purple Heart.[53]

Under current law, and as originally enacted, Section 256(e) of BBEDCA allows a maximum 2% reduction in budget authority for VA medical care for any fiscal year. However, Section 255 of BBEDCA, as amended in 2010 (P.L. 111-139), specifically excludes from sequestration *all* programs administered by the VA, which includes veterans' medical care. This apparent discrepancy between the two sections of the law raised questions about whether VA will be totally exempt from sequestration or whether medical care will be subject to a maximum permissible 2% reduction in budget authority, if a BCA-triggered sequestration occurs as scheduled on January 2, 2013. On April 23, 2012, OMB issued a letter stating that "all programs administered by the VA, including Veterans' Medicare Care, are exempt from sequestration under Section 255(b)."[54] In its report issued pursuant to the Sequestration Transparency Act, OMB further clarified that administration accounts (which include, among others, construction projects, general administration, and information technology systems) are exempt.[55] In other words, all accounts of the Department of Veterans Affairs are exempt from sequestration.

Child Support Enforcement[56]

The Child Support Enforcement (CSE) program is a mandatory spending program that seeks to enhance the well-being of children by obtaining child support, including financial and medical support, from noncustodial parents through services and activities that locate noncustodial parents, establish paternity, establish child support obligations, and collect and monitor child support payments. The CSE program is a federal-state program, administered by HHS. The

---

[50] See discussion on pages 4 and 5 of *OMB Report Pursuant to the Sequestration Transparency Act,* September 2012.

[51] This section was prepared by Sidath Panangala, spanangala@crs.loc.gov, 7-0623.

[52] U.S. Department of Veterans Affairs, *FY 2010 Performance and Accountability Report,* Washington, DC, November 17, 2008, p. I-20. Established on January 3, 1946, as the Department of Medicine and Surgery by P.L. 79-293, succeeded in 1989 by the Veterans Health Services and Research Administration, renamed the Veterans Health Administration in 1991.

[53] For more information on eligibility for VA health care, see CRS Report R42747, *Health Care for Veterans: Answers to Frequently Asked Questions,* by Sidath Viranga Panangala and Erin Bagalman.

[54] Letter from Steven D. Aitken, Deputy General Counsel Office of Management and Budget (OMB), to Julia C. Matta, Assistant General Counsel for Appropriations and Budget, U.S. Government Accountability Office, April 23, 2012, http://www.murray.senate.gov/public/_cache/files/f8868d52-eec0-43a5-b5c8-cecbff4596e/VASequesterQuestion.pdf.

[55] *OMB Report Pursuant to the Sequestration Transparency Act,* September 2012, pp. 160-165.

[56] This section was prepared by Carmen Solomon-Fears, csolomonfears@crs.loc.gov, 7-7306.

federal government reimburses each state for 66% of all expenditures on CSE activities and also provides states with an incentive payment to encourage them to operate effective CSE programs.

Section 256(f) of BBEDCA stipulates that any required reduction in CSE program expenditures or CSE incentive payments must be accomplished by reducing the federal matching rate for state CSE program costs. However, subsequent to enactment of this provision, Section 255 was amended (in 1997, by P.L. 105-33), and specifically excludes from sequestration Family Support Programs, which include the CSE program.

Federal Pay[57]

In general, for purposes of sequestration, Section 256(g) provides that federal pay under a statutory pay system—the General Schedule (GS), Foreign Service (FS) pay schedule, and Department of Medicine and Surgery at the Department of Veterans Affairs (VA) pay schedule— is subject to reduction in the same manner as other administrative expense components of the federal budget (see "Federal Administrative Expenses," immediately below).[58] Likewise, elements of military pay[59] are subject to such reduction. Such an order may not, however, reduce or have the effect of reducing the rate of pay an employee is entitled to under the GS, FS, or VA pay systems or any increase in special pay rates authorized by 5 U.S.C. §5305. The order also may not reduce or have the effect of reducing the rate of any element of military pay an individual is entitled to or any increase in rates of pay authorized by 37 U.S.C. §1009, or any other provision of law.

The conference report (H. Rept. 99-433) that accompanied the original BBEDCA explained the provision as follows:

> The conference agreement provides that rates of pay for civilian employees (and rates of basic pay, basic subsistence allowances and basic quarters allowances for members of the uniformed services) may not be reduced pursuant to a sequestration order. The agreement retains the House position that a scheduled pay increase may not be reduced pursuant to an order and the Federal pay be treated as other components of administrative expenses. The conferees urge program managers to employ all other options available to them in order to achieve savings required under a sequestration order and resort to personnel furloughs only if other methods prove insufficient.[60]

---

[57] This section was prepared by Barbara Schwemle, bschwemle@crs.loc.gov, 7-8655.

[58] Budgetary resources available for federal pay, which would be subject to sequestration as part of the reduction of administrative expenses, are detailed in the September 2012 OMB report issued pursuant to the Sequestration Transparency Act under the "Salaries and Expenses" function for each account.

[59] The term "elements of military pay" means the monthly basic pay adjustments for members of the uniformed services authorized by 37 U.S.C. §1009, allowances provided to members of the uniformed services under 37 U.S.C. §§403a and 405, and cadet pay and midshipman pay under 37 U.S.C. §203(c). The term "uniformed services" means the Army, Navy, Air Force, Marine Corps, Coast Guard, National Oceanic and Atmospheric Administration, and Public Health Service.

[60] *Congressional Record*, vol. 131, December 10, 1985, p. 35776.

Federal Administrative Expenses[61]

In general, under Section 256(h) of BBEDCA, federal administrative expenses are subject to sequestration, regardless of whether they are incurred in connection with a program, project, activity, or account that is otherwise exempt or subject to a special rule.[62] As examples, while Social Security and Supplemental Security Income (SSI) are exempt from sequestration, the federal administrative expenses associated with these programs would generally not be exempt. With regard to the sequester scheduled to take place on January 2, 2013, however, OMB has determined that the special rule for federal administrative expenses applies only to mandatory funds and not discretionary funds.[63] This means, according to OMB, that mandatory administrative expenses for an otherwise exempt program are subject to sequestration, but that discretionary administrative expenses for an exempt program are not. Therefore, since federal administrative expenses for Social Security and SSI are discretionary (although program benefits are mandatory), they would not be subject to sequestration on January 2, 2013, despite the special rule described above.

Section 256 also states that federal payments to state and local governments that match or reimburse these governments for their administrative costs are not considered "federal administrative expenses" and are subject to sequestration *only* to the extent that the relevant federal program is subject to sequestration. In other words, if a program is exempt under Section 255, then federal payments to states for the costs of administering that program also are exempt. (However, certain unemployment compensation payments are not covered by this provision, as noted below.)

Unemployment Compensation[64]

Section 256(i) of the BBEDCA reiterates the exemption from sequestration (provided under Section 255) of federal loans to the states for payment of unemployment benefits. Additionally, Section 256(i) exempts regular unemployment compensation (UC) benefits from sequestration. This exemption is extended to UC for former federal workers (UCFE) and UC for former servicemembers (UCX). Generally, these benefits have a duration of up to 26 weeks and are paid by state unemployment taxes. However, Section 256 specifically does not exempt administrative grants to the states and the federal share of the permanently authorized extended benefit (EB) program from sequestration. States would be required to continue to pay their share of EB payments. If a state's unemployment insurance law allows it, the state may reduce the EB benefit amount by a percentage that does not exceed the percentage by which the federal share of EB has been reduced. The current authorization of the temporary emergency unemployment compensation (EUC08) benefit ends at the end of calendar year 2012. If the authorization of the EUC08 benefit were extended, the EUC08 benefit would be subject to sequestration unless new legislation directing a different treatment were to be enacted.

---

[61] The BBEDCA does not define administrative expenses. For purposes of its report issued pursuant to the Sequestration Transparency Act, OMB states that "'administrative expenses' for typical government programs are defined as the object classes for personnel compensation, travel, transportation, communication, equipment, supplies, materials, and other services."

[62] The statute lists several federal financial services entities that would not be covered by this section (e.g., Comptroller of the Currency, Federal Deposit Insurance Corporation, and others).

[63] See discussion on pp. 4-5 of *OMB Report Pursuant to the Sequestration Transparency Act,* September 2012.

[64] This section was prepared by Julie Whittaker, jwhittaker@crs.loc.gov, 7-2587.

Commodity Credit Corporation[65]

The Commodity Credit Corporation (CCC) is the funding mechanism for the mandatory spending of the U.S. Department of Agriculture (USDA) for farm commodity support and certain conservation programs. The CCC is a wholly owned government corporation that has the legal authority to borrow up to $30 billion at any one time from the U.S. Treasury. Its borrowing authority is replenished annually in the Agriculture appropriations bill by a "such sums as are necessary" appropriation. Most spending for these programs was authorized by the 2008 farm bill (P.L. 110-246).

Section 256(j) says that sequestration should not restrict the CCC's authority to discharge its primary duties. Specifically, it states that commodity loan contracts entered into before the sequestration order shall not be reduced.[66] Section 256 says, though, that loan contracts after the sequestration order shall be reduced. The farm commodity programs have evolved to include other support mechanisms than the loan program, and the loan program is no longer the primary outlay. It is unclear whether the Section 256 special rule applies to any of the more recent farm commodity, conservation, and other programs that are funded by the CCC.

---

[65] This section was prepared by Jim Monke, jmonke@crs.loc.gov, 7-9664.

[66] Commodity loans are one part of the farm support program that makes government loans to farmers at farm-bill specified support prices per unit of commodity. Farmers can use these loans as financing to pay their expenses and, if market prices are below the support price, can benefit financially by the difference between the support price and the market price. Outlays of the federal crop insurance program are not funded under the CCC but instead have their own mandatory funding mechanism, addressed in Section 255, that exempts the prior legal obligations of the Federal Crop Insurance Fund from sequestration.

Appendix. Section 255 of the Balanced Budget and Emergency Deficit Control Act, as Amended

SEC. 255. (2 U.S.C. 905) EXEMPT PROGRAMS AND ACTIVITIES.

(a) SOCIAL SECURITY BENEFITS AND TIER I RAILROAD RETIREMENT

BENEFITS.—Benefits payable under the old-age, survivors, and disability insurance program established under title II of the Social Security Act (42 U.S.C. 401 et seq.), and benefits payable under section 231b(a), 231b(f)(2), 231c(a), and 231c(f) of title 45 United States Code, shall be exempt from reduction under any order issued under this part.

(b) VETERANS PROGRAMS.—The following programs shall be exempt from reduction under any order issued under this part:

All programs administered by the Department of Veterans Affairs.

Special Benefits for Certain World War II Veterans (28–0401–0–1–701).

(c) NET INTEREST.—No reduction of payments for net interest (all of major functional category 900) shall be made under any order issued under this part.

(d) REFUNDABLE INCOME TAX CREDITS.—Payments to individuals made pursuant to provisions of the Internal Revenue Code of 1986 establishing refundable tax credits shall be exempt from reduction under any order issued under this part.

(e) NON-DEFENSE UNOBLIGATED BALANCES.—Unobligated balances of budget authority carried over from prior fiscal years, except balances in the defense category, shall be exempt from reduction under any order issued under this part.

(f) OPTIONAL EXEMPTION OF MILITARY PERSONNEL.—

(1) IN GENERAL.—The President may, with respect to any military personnel account, exempt that account from sequestration or provide for a lower uniform percentage reduction than would otherwise apply.

(2) LIMITATION.—The President may not use the authority provided by paragraph (1) unless the President notifies the Congress of the manner in which such authority will be exercised on or before the date specified in section 254(a) for the budget year.

(g) OTHER PROGRAMS AND ACTIVITIES.—

(1)(A) The following budget accounts and activities shall be exempt from reduction under any order issued under this part:

Activities resulting from private donations, bequests, or voluntary contributions to the Government.

Activities financed by voluntary payments to the Government for goods or services to be provided for such payments.

Administration of Territories, Northern Mariana Islands Covenant grants (14–0412–0–1–808).

Advances to the Unemployment Trust Fund and Other Funds (16–0327–0–1–600).

Black Lung Disability Trust Fund Refinancing (16–0329–0–1–601).

Bonneville Power Administration Fund and borrowing authority established pursuant to section 13 of Public Law 93–454 (1974), as amended (89–4045–0–3–271).

Claims, Judgments, and Relief Acts (20–1895–0–1–808).

Compact of Free Association (14–0415–0–1–808).

Compensation of the President (11–0209–01–1–802).

Comptroller of the Currency, Assessment Funds (20–8413–0–8–373).

Continuing Fund, Southeastern Power Administration (89–5653–0–2–271).

Continuing Fund, Southwestern Power Administration (89–5649–0–2–271).

Dual Benefits Payments Account (60–0111–0–1–601).

Emergency Fund, Western Area Power Administration (89–5069–0–2–271).

Exchange Stabilization Fund (20–4444–0–3–155).

Farm Credit Administration Operating Expenses Fund (78–4131–0–3–351).

Farm Credit System Insurance Corporation, Farm Credit Insurance Fund (78–4171–0–3–351).

Federal Deposit Insurance Corporation, Deposit Insurance Fund (51–4596–0–4–373).

Federal Deposit Insurance Corporation, FSLIC Resolution Fund (51–4065–0–3–373).

Federal Deposit Insurance Corporation, Noninterest Bearing Transaction Account Guarantee (51–4458–0–3–373).

Federal Deposit Insurance Corporation, Senior Unsecured Debt Guarantee (51–4457–0–3–373).

Federal Home Loan Mortgage Corporation (Freddie Mac).

Federal Housing Finance Agency, Administrative Expenses (95–5532–0–2–371).

Federal National Mortgage Corporation (Fannie Mae).

Federal Payment to the District of Columbia Judicial Retirement and Survivors Annuity Fund (20–1713–0–1–752).

Federal Payment to the District of Columbia Pension Fund (20–1714–0–1–601).

Federal Payments to the Railroad Retirement Accounts (60–0113–0–1–601).

Federal Reserve Bank Reimbursement Fund (20–1884–0–1–803).

Financial Agent Services (20–1802–0–1–803).

Foreign Military Sales Trust Fund (11–8242–0–7–155).

Hazardous Waste Management, Conservation Reserve Program (12–4336–0–3–999).

Host Nation Support Fund for Relocation (97–8337–0–7–051).

Internal Revenue Collections for Puerto Rico (20–5737–0–2–806).

Intragovernmental funds, including those from which the outlays are derived primarily from resources paid in from other government accounts, except to the extent such funds are augmented by direct appropriations for the fiscal year during which an order is in effect.

Medical Facilities Guarantee and Loan Fund (75–9931–0–3–551).

National Credit Union Administration, Central Liquidity Facility (25–4470–0–3–373).

National Credit Union Administration, Corporate Credit Union Share Guarantee Program (25–4476–0–3–376).

National Credit Union Administration, Credit Union Homeowners Affordability Relief Program (25–4473–0–3–371).

National Credit Union Administration, Credit Union Share Insurance Fund (25–4468–0–3–373).

National Credit Union Administration, Credit Union System Investment Program (25–4474–0–3–376).

National Credit Union Administration, Operating fund (25–4056–0–3–373).

National Credit Union Administration, Share Insurance Fund Corporate Debt Guarantee Program (25–4469–0–3–376).

National Credit Union Administration, U.S. Central Federal Credit Union Capital Program (25–4475–0–3–376).

Office of Thrift Supervision (20–4108–0–3–373).

Panama Canal Commission Compensation Fund (16–5155–0–2–602).

Payment of Vietnam and USS Pueblo prisoner-of-war claims within the Salaries and Expenses, Foreign Claims Settlement account (15–0100–0–1–153).

Payment to Civil Service Retirement and Disability Fund (24–0200–0–1–805).

Payment to Department of Defense Medicare-Eligible Retiree Health Care Fund (97–0850–0–1–054).

Payment to Judiciary Trust Funds (10–0941–0–1–752).

Payment to Military Retirement Fund (97–0040–0–1–054).

Payment to the Foreign Service Retirement and Disability Fund (19–0540–0–1–153).

Payments to Copyright Owners (03–5175–0–2–376).

Payments to Health Care Trust Funds (75–0580–0–1–571).

Payment to Radiation Exposure Compensation Trust Fund (15–0333–0–1–054).

Payments to Social Security Trust Funds (28–0404–0–1–651).

Payments to the United States Territories, Fiscal Assistance (14–0418–0–1–806).

Payments to trust funds from excise taxes or other receipts properly creditable to such trust funds.

Payments to widows and heirs of deceased Members of Congress (00–0215–0–1–801).

Postal Service Fund (18–4020–0–3–372).

Radiation Exposure Compensation Trust Fund (15–8116–0–1–054).

Reimbursement to Federal Reserve Banks (20–0562–0–1–803).

Salaries of Article III judges.

Soldiers and Airmen's Home, payment of claims (84–8930–0–7–705).

Tennessee Valley Authority Fund, except nonpower programs and activities (64–4110–0–3–999).

Tribal and Indian trust accounts within the Department of the Interior which fund prior legal obligations of the Government or which are established pursuant to Acts of Congress regarding Federal management of tribal real property or other fiduciary responsibilities, including but not limited to Tribal Special Fund (14–5265–0–2–452),

Tribal Trust Fund (14–8030–0–7–452),

White Earth Settlement (14–2204–0–1–452), and Indian Water Rights and Habitat Acquisition (14–5505–0–2–303).

United Mine Workers of America 1992 Benefit Plan (95–8260–0–7–551).

United Mine Workers of America 1993 Benefit Plan (95–8535–0–7–551).

United Mine Workers of America Combined Benefit Fund (95–8295–0–7–551).

United States Enrichment Corporation Fund (95–4054–0–3–271).

Universal Service Fund (27–5183–0–2–376).

Vaccine Injury Compensation (75–0320–0–1–551).

Vaccine Injury Compensation Program Trust Fund (20–8175–0–7–551).

(B) The following Federal retirement and disability accounts and activities shall be exempt from reduction under any order issued under this part:

Black Lung Disability Trust Fund (20–8144–0–7–601).

Central Intelligence Agency Retirement and Disability System Fund (56–3400–0–1–054).

Civil Service Retirement and Disability Fund (24–8135–0–7–602).

Comptrollers general retirement system (05–0107–0–1–801).

Contributions to U.S. Park Police annuity benefits, Other Permanent Appropriations (14–9924–0–2–303).

Court of Appeals for Veterans Claims Retirement Fund (95–8290–0–7–705).

Department of Defense Medicare-Eligible Retiree Health Care Fund (97–5472–0–2–551).

District of Columbia Federal Pension Fund (20–5511–0–2–601).

District of Columbia Judicial Retirement and Survivors Annuity Fund (20–8212–0–7–602).

Energy Employees Occupational Illness Compensation Fund (16–1523–0–1–053).

Foreign National Employees Separation Pay (97–8165–0–7–051).

Foreign Service National Defined Contributions Retirement Fund (19–5497–0–2–602).

Foreign Service National Separation Liability Trust Fund (19–8340–0–7–602).

Foreign Service Retirement and Disability Fund (19–8186–0–7–602).

Government Payment for Annuitants, Employees Health Benefits (24–0206–0–1–551).

Government Payment for Annuitants, Employee Life Insurance (24–0500–0–1–602).

Judicial Officers' Retirement Fund (10–8122–0–7–602).

Judicial Survivors' Annuities Fund (10–8110–0–7–602).

Military Retirement Fund (97–8097–0–7–602).

National Railroad Retirement Investment Trust (60–8118–0–7–601).

National Oceanic and Atmospheric Administration retirement (13–1450–0–1–306).

Pensions for former Presidents (47–0105–0–1–802).

Postal Service Retiree Health Benefits Fund (24–5391–0–2–551).

Public Safety Officer Benefits (15–0403–0–1–754).

Rail Industry Pension Fund (60–8011–0–7–601).

Retired Pay, Coast Guard (70–0602–0–1–403).

Retirement Pay and Medical Benefits for Commissioned Officers, Public Health Service (75–0379–0–1–551).

Special Benefits for Disabled Coal Miners (16–0169–0–1–601).

Special Benefits, Federal Employees' Compensation Act (16–1521–0–1–600).

Special Workers Compensation Expenses (16–9971–0–7–601).

Tax Court Judges Survivors Annuity Fund (23–8115–0–7–602).

United States Court of Federal Claims Judges' Retirement Fund (10–8124–0–7–602).

United States Secret Service, DC Annuity (70–0400–0–1–751).

Voluntary Separation Incentive Fund (97–8335–0–7–051).

(2) Prior legal obligations of the Government in the following budget accounts and activities shall be exempt from any order issued under this part:

Biomass Energy Development (20–0114–0–1–271).

Check Forgery Insurance Fund (20–4109–0–3–803).

Credit liquidating accounts.

Credit reestimates.

Employees Life Insurance Fund (24–8424–0–8–602).

Federal Aviation Insurance Revolving Fund (69–4120– 0–3–402).

Federal Crop Insurance Corporation Fund (12–4085–0–3–351).

Federal Emergency Management Agency, National Flood Insurance Fund (58–4236–0–3–453).

Geothermal resources development fund (89–0206–0–1–271).

Low-Rent Public Housing—Loans and Other Expenses (86–4098–0–3–604).

Maritime Administration, War Risk Insurance Revolving Fund (69–4302–0–3–403).

Natural Resource Damage Assessment Fund (14–1618–0–1–302).

Overseas Private Investment Corporation, Noncredit Account (71–4184–0–3–151).

Pension Benefit Guaranty Corporation Fund (16–4204–0–3–601).

San Joaquin Restoration Fund (14–5537–0–2–301).

Servicemembers' Group Life Insurance Fund (36–4009–0–3–701).

Terrorism Insurance Program (20–0123–0–1–376).

(h) LOW-INCOME PROGRAMS.—The following programs shall be exempt from reduction under any order issued under this part:

Academic Competitiveness/Smart Grant Program (91–0205–0–1–502).

Child Care Entitlement to States (75–1550–0–1–609).

Child Enrollment Contingency Fund (75–5551–0–2–551).

Child Nutrition Programs (with the exception of special milk programs) (12–3539–0–1–605).

Children's Health Insurance Fund (75–0515–0–1–551).

Commodity Supplemental Food Program (12–3507–0–1–605).

Contingency Fund (75–1522–0–1–609).

Family Support Programs (75–1501–0–1–609).

Federal Pell Grants under section 401 Title IV of the Higher Education Act.

Grants to States for Medicaid (75–0512–0–1–551).

Payments for Foster Care and Permanency (75–1545–0–1–609).

Supplemental Nutrition Assistance Program (12–3505–0–1–605).

Supplemental Security Income Program (28–0406–0–1–609).

Temporary Assistance for Needy Families (75–1552–0–1–609).

(i) ECONOMIC RECOVERY PROGRAMS.—The following programs shall be exempt from reduction under any order issued under this part:

GSE Preferred Stock Purchase Agreements (20–0125–0–1–371).

Office of Financial Stability (20–0128–0–1–376).

Special Inspector General for the Troubled Asset Relief Program (20–0133–0–1–376).

(j) SPLIT TREATMENT PROGRAMS.—Each of the following programs shall be exempt from any order under this part to the extent that the budgetary resources of such programs are subject to obligation limitations in appropriations bills:

Federal-Aid Highways (69–8083–0–7–401).

Highway Traffic Safety Grants (69–8020–0–7–401).

Operations and Research NHTSA and National Driver Register (69–8016–0–7–401).

Motor Carrier Safety Operations and Programs (69–8159–0–7–401).

Motor Carrier Safety Grants (69–8158–0–7–401).

Formula and Bus Grants (69–8350–0–7–401).

Grants-In-Aid for Airports (69–8106–0–7–402).

(j) IDENTIFICATION OF PROGRAMS.—For purposes of subsections (b), (g), and (h), each account is identified by the designated budget account identification code number set forth in the Budget of the United States Government 2010–Appendix, and an activity within an account is designated by the name of the activity and the identification code number of the account.

SEC. 256. (2 U.S.C. 906) [excerpt]

(7) EXEMPTIONS FROM SEQUESTRATION.—In addition to the programs and activities specified in section 255, the following shall be exempt from sequestration under this part:

(A) PART D LOW-INCOME SUBSIDIES.—Premium and cost-sharing subsidies under section 1860D–14 of the Social Security Act.

(B) PART D CATASTROPHIC SUBSIDY.—Payments under section 1860D–15(b) and (e)(2)(B) of the Social Security Act.

(C) QUALIFIED INDIVIDUAL (QI) PREMIUMS.—Payments to States for coverage of Medicare cost-sharing for certain low-income Medicare beneficiaries under section 1933 of the Social Security Act.

Author Contact Information

Karen Spar, Coordinator
Specialist in Domestic Social Policy and Division
Research Coordinator
kspar@crs.loc.gov, 7-7319

Patricia A. Davis
Specialist in Health Care Financing
pdavis@crs.loc.gov, 7-7362

Elayne J. Heisler
Analyst in Health Services
eheisler@crs.loc.gov, 7-4453

Jim Monke
Specialist in Agricultural Policy
jmonke@crs.loc.gov, 7-9664

Sidath Viranga Panangala
Specialist in Veterans Policy
spanangala@crs.loc.gov, 7-0623

Barbara L. Schwemle
Analyst in American National Government
bschwemle@crs.loc.gov, 7-8655

David P. Smole
Specialist in Education Policy
dsmole@crs.loc.gov, 7-0624

Carmen Solomon-Fears
Specialist in Social Policy
csolomonfears@crs.loc.gov, 7-7306

Julie M. Whittaker
Specialist in Income Security
jwhittaker@crs.loc.gov, 7-2587

Acknowledgments

The coordinator of this report appreciates the helpful comments received from Bill Heniff Jr., Analyst on Congress and the Legislative Process, and Todd Tatelman, (now former) Legislative Attorney.

www.ingramcontent.com/pod-product-compliance
Lightning Source LLC
Chambersburg PA
CBHW080750290526
45790CB00008B/3395

* 9 7 8 1 4 8 1 0 7 0 7 2 0 *

SEC. 256. (2 U.S.C. 906) [excerpt]

(7) EXEMPTIONS FROM SEQUESTRATION.—In addition to the programs and activities specified in section 255, the following shall be exempt from sequestration under this part:

(A) PART D LOW-INCOME SUBSIDIES.—Premium and cost-sharing subsidies under section 1860D–14 of the Social Security Act.

(B) PART D CATASTROPHIC SUBSIDY.—Payments under section 1860D–15(b) and (e)(2)(B) of the Social Security Act.

(C) QUALIFIED INDIVIDUAL (QI) PREMIUMS.—Payments to States for coverage of Medicare cost-sharing for certain low-income Medicare beneficiaries under section 1933 of the Social Security Act.

Author Contact Information

Karen Spar, Coordinator
Specialist in Domestic Social Policy and Division Research Coordinator
kspar@crs.loc.gov, 7-7319

Patricia A. Davis
Specialist in Health Care Financing
pdavis@crs.loc.gov, 7-7362

Elayne J. Heisler
Analyst in Health Services
eheisler@crs.loc.gov, 7-4453

Jim Monke
Specialist in Agricultural Policy
jmonke@crs.loc.gov, 7-9664

Sidath Viranga Panangala
Specialist in Veterans Policy
spanangala@crs.loc.gov, 7-0623

Barbara L. Schwemle
Analyst in American National Government
bschwemle@crs.loc.gov, 7-8655

David P. Smole
Specialist in Education Policy
dsmole@crs.loc.gov, 7-0624

Carmen Solomon-Fears
Specialist in Social Policy
csolomonfears@crs.loc.gov, 7-7306

Julie M. Whittaker
Specialist in Income Security
jwhittaker@crs.loc.gov, 7-2587

Acknowledgments

The coordinator of this report appreciates the helpful comments received from Bill Heniff Jr., Analyst on Congress and the Legislative Process, and Todd Tatelman, (now former) Legislative Attorney.

www.ingramcontent.com/pod-product-compliance
Lightning Source LLC
Chambersburg PA
CBHW080750290526
45790CB00008B/3395